First edition 2023

Contents

Introduction: Understanding Affiliate Marketing

Affiliate marketing is a powerful and increasingly popular way for brands to promote their products or services online. In this introductory chapter, we'll provide an overview of what affiliate marketing is, how it works, and why it is such a powerful and measurable acquisition tool for brands.

Affiliate marketing is a form of online advertising where brands (known as advertisers) partner with third-party websites (known as publishers) to promote their products or services. The advertiser provides the publisher with a unique link or code that they can use to direct their audience to the advertiser's website. If the publisher's audience clicks on the link and makes a purchase on the advertiser's website, the publishers receive a commission on the sale.

Affiliate marketing offers many benefits to brands with an online presence. Firstly, it provides a cost-effective way to reach a wider audience and drive sales. By partnering with relevant and reputable publishers, brands can tap into existing communities of potential customers and benefit from their trust and loyalty. Secondly, affiliate marketing offers a way to track and measure the effectiveness of advertising campaigns with precision, allowing brands to optimise their strategies for maximum ROI. Finally, affiliate marketing can help to build long-term partnerships with publishers who can become valuable brand advocates and ambassadors.

However, launching a successful affiliate program in the requires careful planning and execution. Brands need to identify the right publishers to partner with, establish clear terms and goals for their program, and build effective communication and support systems to foster strong relationships with their partners. Additionally, brands need to be aware of the specific legal and regulatory requirements that apply to affiliate marketing in their country of residence, in the UK this would include Advertising Standards Authority (ASA) guidelines on online advertising and the General Data Protection Regulation (GDPR) rules on data protection.

In the following chapters, we'll dive into the specific strategies and tactics that brands can use to launch and manage successful affiliate programs. By understanding the fundamentals of affiliate marketing and the unique challenges and opportunities of the affiliate market industry, you'll be well-equipped to build a thriving affiliate program that delivers for your brand.

Chapter 1: Setting Up Your Brand for Affiliate Success - Strategies for Branding, Marketing, and Online Presence

In order to successfully launch and run an affiliate program, it's essential to establish a strong brand identity and online presence that will attract and engage potential publishers. Here are some key strategies for setting up your brand for affiliate success:

Define Your Brand Identity

Defining your brand identity is a crucial step in creating a successful affiliate marketing program. It requires establishing a unique and consistent image of your brand that resonates with your target audience. A strong brand identity helps differentiate you from your competitors and makes your brand easily recognisable.

To define your brand identity, you need to consider several key elements. Firstly, your brand values should be established, which are the principles and beliefs that guide your brand's behaviour and decisions. These values should be in sync with your target audience's values and conveyed throughout your brand, including your affiliate program.

Your brand voice is also essential, which is the tone and language used in your messaging. It should be consistent across all channels and reflect your brand's personality. It can be professional, conversational, humorous, or any other tone that resonates with your target audience.

Your brand's visual identity is another vital element to consider, which includes your logo, colour palette, typography, and any visual elements used in your marketing materials. It should be consistent across all platforms, including your website, social media, and affiliate program. Your visual identity should reflect your brand values and personality and be designed to appeal to your target audience.

Your brand messaging is also critical. It should be clear, concise, and consistent across all platforms. It should convey your brand's unique value proposition and be tailored to your target audience's needs and preferences. Your messaging should also be reflected in your affiliate program, with clear guidelines for affiliate promotions and messaging.

Finally, your brand story is the narrative that connects your brand with your target audience. It should include your brand's history, mission, and values, and be communicated in all aspects of your brand, including your affiliate program. Your brand story should be designed to resonate with your target audience and create a sense of connection and loyalty.

Once you have defined your brand identity, it's important to ensure that it's reflected in all aspects of your affiliate program. This includes clear guidelines for affiliate promotions and messaging, consistent visual branding, and a strong brand voice in all affiliate communications.

Develop Your Branding

Once you have a clear brand identity, it's important to develop a consistent and compelling branding strategy across all channels. This includes your website, social media profiles, email marketing campaigns, and any other digital marketing.

To develop your brand, you need to ensure that your brand's visual identity is consistent across all platforms. This includes your logo, colour palette, typography, and any visual elements used in your marketing materials. Your brand's visual identity should be designed to appeal to your target audience and reflect your brand's personality and values.

Your website is a crucial component of your branding strategy, and it should reflect your brand's visual identity and messaging. It should be user-friendly, visually appealing, and provide a seamless user experience. Your website should also be optimised for search engines, making it easy for your target audience to find you online.

Social media is another essential channel for your branding strategy. Your social media profiles should reflect your brand's visual identity and messaging and be tailored to each platform. You should also develop a social media content strategy that aligns with your brand's values and resonates with your target audience.

Email marketing campaigns can also be an effective tool for your branding strategy. Your emails should reflect your brand's visual identity and messaging and be designed to engage your target audience. You should also segment your email list based on your target audience's preferences and needs, delivering personalised and relevant content.

In addition to digital marketing, your branding strategy should extend to other areas of your business. This includes your customer service, packaging, and any other touchpoints where your brand interacts with your target audience.

By developing a consistent and compelling branding strategy across all channels, you can strengthen your brand's image and increase brand loyalty.

Optimise Your Website

Your website is your most important digital asset and the primary point of contact for potential publishers. Make sure your website is user-friendly, visually appealing, and optimised for search engines (SEO).

A user-friendly website is essential for a successful affiliate marketing program. Your website should be easy to navigate, with clear calls to action (CTAs) and relevant content that engages your target audience. It should also be mobile-friendly, as more and more users access the internet on their smartphones.

Your website's design should also be visually appealing and reflect your brand's visual identity. This includes your logo, colour palette, typography, and any visual elements used in your marketing materials. By maintaining a consistent visual identity across all platforms, you can increase brand recognition and build brand loyalty.

Search engine optimisation (SEO) is another crucial element of your website's optimisation. SEO is the process of optimising your website to rank higher in search engine results pages (SERPs) for relevant keywords. This can help increase your website's visibility and drive more traffic to your website.

To optimise your website for SEO, start by conducting keyword research to identify the keywords and phrases your target audience is searching for. Then, optimise your website's content, meta descriptions, and page titles to include these keywords. You should also ensure your website's pages load quickly and include high-quality, relevant content.

In addition to optimising your website's content for SEO, it's also important to ensure that your website is technically optimised. This includes optimising your website's images, using header tags correctly, and ensuring your website is mobile-friendly.

By optimising your website for user experience and search engines, you can increase traffic to your website, improve brand recognition, and drive more conversions.

Leverage Social Media

Social media can be a powerful tool for building brand awareness and engaging with potential publishers. Make sure you have an active presence on relevant social media platforms and create content that aligns with your brand values and affiliate program goals.

To leverage social media, start by identifying the platforms your target audience is most active on. For example, if you're targeting a younger audience, you may want to focus on Instagram and TikTok. If you're targeting professionals, LinkedIn may be a better platform for your brand.

Once you've identified the relevant platforms, create a social media strategy that aligns with your brand's values and affiliate program goals. This should include a content plan that includes a mix of promotional content, educational content, and engaging content that resonates with your target audience.

Your social media content should be visually appealing and consistent with your brand's visual identity. Use high-quality images and videos that capture your brand's personality and values. Don't be afraid to experiment with different types of content, such as Instagram Reels or TikTok videos, to see what resonates best with your target audience.

Social media is also a great tool for engaging with your target audience and potential publishers. Respond to comments and messages in a timely manner and use social media listening tools to monitor conversations about your brand and industry. This can help you identify new opportunities and address any concerns or issues in a timely manner.

Finally, make sure you're tracking your social media metrics and adjusting your strategy accordingly. This includes tracking engagement rates, click-through rates, and follower growth. Use this data to optimise your social media strategy and improve your affiliate program's performance.

By leveraging social media, you can increase brand awareness, engage with potential publishers, and drive more traffic to your website.

Participate in Industry Events

Attending industry events and conferences can help you build relationships with potential publishers, learn about new trends and best practices, and establish your brand as a thought leader in your industry.

Industry events and conferences provide an opportunity to network with potential publishers and other industry professionals. You can use these events to build relationships and establish connections with publishers that may be interested in joining your affiliate program. You can also meet other industry professionals who can provide valuable insights and advice on how to improve your affiliate program's performance.

Attending industry events and conferences also allows you to stay up to date with the latest trends and best practices in your industry. You can attend workshops, seminars, and panel discussions to learn about new technologies, marketing strategies, and industry trends. This knowledge can help you optimise your affiliate program and stay ahead of the competition.

Finally, participating in industry events and conferences can help establish your brand as a thought leader in your industry. By speaking at events or participating in panel discussions, you can showcase your brand's expertise and knowledge. This can help build trust with potential publishers and establish your brand as a go-to resource in your industry.

To participate in industry events and conferences, start by identifying the relevant events in your industry. This can include trade shows, conferences, and networking events. Research the events to determine which ones align with your brand's goals and values, and plan to attend those events.

When attending events, make sure you're prepared with business cards and any relevant marketing materials. Be approachable and engage with other attendees to build relationships and establish connections. Finally, follow up with any potential publishers or industry professionals you meet to continue building those relationships.

Chapter 2: The Importance of Conducting a Commercial Viability Check Before Launching an Affiliate Program

When launching an affiliate program, it's important to ensure that your brand has the necessary profit margin available to pay publisher commissions on sales. Conducting a commercial viability check can help you determine whether your brand can sustain an affiliate program and generate a return on investment. Here are some key reasons why conducting a commercial viability check is important:

Ensures Sustainable Profitability

Conducting a commercial viability check helps you determine if your brand can generate sustainable profitability while paying commissions to publishers. If you find that your profit margins are too narrow or that you can't generate enough sales volume to sustain the program, it may be better to delay or adjust your affiliate program launch.

An affiliate program can be a great way to increase sales and grow your brand, but it's important to ensure that the program is financially viable. By conducting a commercial viability check, you can analyse your brand's profitability and determine if it can support the costs of an affiliate program.

To conduct a commercial viability check, start by analysing your current profit margins and projected revenue streams. Determine how much commission you can afford to pay publishers while still maintaining a healthy profit margin. You'll also want to factor in any additional costs associated with running an affiliate program, such as software, tracking, and management fees.

Next, consider the potential sales volume that your affiliate program can generate. Analyse your target audience, the competition, and any potential barriers to sales. This will help you determine if there is enough demand for your product or service to sustain the program.

If you find that your brand can't generate sustainable profitability while paying commissions to publishers, it may be better to delay or adjust your affiliate program launch. This could mean revising your commission structure, adjusting your pricing, or rethinking your marketing strategy.

Launching an affiliate program without conducting a commercial viability check can lead to financial instability and harm your brand's reputation. Publishers may lose trust in your brand if they feel they aren't being adequately compensated, and you may struggle to maintain profitability.

Helps with Budgeting

A commercial viability check helps you establish a budget for your affiliate program. This includes determining the commission rates you can afford to pay publishers while also accounting for other program-related expenses, such as software or staff costs.

Budgeting is an important part of any business strategy, and affiliate marketing is no exception. By conducting a commercial viability check, you can determine the commission rates that will attract publishers while still maintaining a healthy profit margin.

To establish a budget for your affiliate program, start by analysing your current revenue streams and projected growth. Determine how much you can afford to spend on commissions without compromising your profit margins. Keep in mind that the commission rates you offer may depend on the type of products or services you offer, as well as the competition within your industry.

Once you have established your commission rates, you'll want to account for other program-related expenses. This may include software costs for tracking and managing your program, as well as staff costs for dedicated affiliate managers or marketing specialists.

By establishing a clear budget for your affiliate program, you can avoid overspending and ensure that your program is financially sustainable. This will help you attract high-quality publishers and maintain a positive reputation within the industry.

Furthermore, a commercial viability check can help you adjust your budget as needed. As your program grows, you may need to increase your commission rates or allocate more resources to your affiliate team. By regularly conducting viability checks, you can ensure that your program remains profitable and scalable.

Helps Identify Areas for Improvement

Conducting a commercial viability check helps you identify areas where your brand can improve profitability. For example, you may find that your current pricing strategy doesn't leave enough room for commissions, or that your conversion rates need to be improved.

By analysing your revenue streams and projected growth, you can identify potential areas where your affiliate program could benefit from improvement. This includes examining your pricing strategy and determining whether there is enough margin to pay commissions to publishers.

You may also want to evaluate your conversion rates and identify any areas where you can improve. This may involve optimising your website for conversions, refining your sales funnel, or testing new marketing strategies.

A commercial viability check can also help you identify any operational inefficiencies that could impact the profitability of your affiliate program. For example, you may find that your program's tracking software is not accurate, or that you need additional staff to manage the program effectively.

By identifying areas for improvement, you can make informed decisions on how to optimise your affiliate program and maximise profitability. This may involve adjusting your pricing strategy, investing in new marketing channels, or upgrading your program's tracking software.

Regularly conducting commercial viability checks can help you stay on top of your program's profitability and identify opportunities for growth. By constantly analysing your program's performance, you can make informed decisions that will help you improve profitability and maintain a sustainable program.

Minimises Risk

Launching an affiliate program without conducting a commercial viability check can be risky. If you are unable to pay commissions to publishers or sustain the program in the long-term, you risk damaging relationships with publishers and tarnishing your brand's reputation in the affiliate industry.

By conducting a commercial viability check, you can minimise this risk by identifying potential issues before they become a problem. For example, if you find that your profit margins are too narrow to pay commissions to publishers, you can delay the program's launch until you can improve profitability.

Conducting a commercial viability check can also help you identify potential legal or compliance issues that could arise if you launch an affiliate program without proper preparation. For example, if you are offering incentives to publishers that violate industry regulations, you risk legal action and damage to your brand's reputation.

By minimising risk through a commercial viability check, you can ensure that your affiliate program is compliant with industry regulations, sustainable in the long-term, and attractive to quality publishers. This will help you build a positive reputation in the industry and establish a successful affiliate program.

Chapter 3: The Value of Competitor Analysis in Developing an Affiliate Program

When developing an affiliate program, it's important to conduct competitor analysis to gain insights into what works in the market and how you can differentiate your program. Analysing your competitors' affiliate programs can provide valuable information that can help you create a more effective and profitable program. Here are some key reasons why competitor analysis is important for developing an affiliate program:

Identify Best Practices

Analysing your competitors' affiliate programs can help you identify best practices and strategies that have been successful in the market. This can help you develop a program that is optimised for success and has a higher chance of attracting publishers.

By analysing the programs of your competitors, you can gain insight into what commission rates they offer, how they structure their program, and what types of publishers they work with. This information can help you determine the most effective strategies for your own program, including what commission rates to offer and what types of publishers to target.

Furthermore, competitor analysis can help you identify areas where you can differentiate your program from those of your competitors. For example, you may find that your competitors do not offer support for publishers, or that they have a limited selection of products to promote. By identifying these areas, you can develop a program that offers more value to publishers and stands out in the market.

Additionally, competitor analysis can help you identify gaps in the market that your brand can fill. By identifying niches that are not currently being served by your competitors, you can develop a program that caters to these niches and attracts publishers that are interested in promoting products in these areas.

Understand Commission Structures

Understanding your competitors' commission structures can help you set your own commission rates competitively, so you can attract publishers while remaining profitable.

By analysing your competitors' commission rates, you can gain insight into what rates are currently being offered in your industry. This information can help you determine what rates are competitive and attractive to publishers, while still allowing you to generate a profit.

Furthermore, understanding your competitors' commission structures can help you identify the types of performance incentives that are being offered. This includes bonuses for high-performing publishers, increased commission rates for achieving certain milestones, and other rewards that motivate publishers to perform well.

By understanding these structures, you can develop a commission structure that is attractive to publishers and incentivises them to perform well. This can help you attract quality publishers and generate sustainable revenue for your brand.

It's important to note, however, that commission rates are not the only factor that publishers consider when deciding whether to join an affiliate program. Publishers also consider the quality of the products and services being offered, the level of support provided by the brand, and the overall reputation of the brand.

Therefore, while understanding your competitors' commission structures is important, it's just one aspect of developing a successful affiliate program. It's equally important to offer high-quality products and services, provide excellent support to publishers, and build a strong reputation in the market. By doing so, you can attract quality publishers and generate sustainable revenue for your brand.

Analyse Promotions

Analysing your competitors' promotional strategies can provide valuable insights into what works well in the market and what types of promotions publishers are most likely to respond to. By examining the promotions of successful affiliate programs in your industry, you can gain a better understanding of how to structure your own promotions to attract publishers and drive sales.

Some questions to consider when analysing your competitors' promotions might include:

- What types of promotions are they offering? Are they offering exclusive discounts or coupon codes, or are they running promotions such as free shipping or bonus items with a purchase?

- How frequently are they running promotions? Are they running promotions on a regular basis, or only during certain times of the year?

- How are they promoting their promotions? Are they using email marketing, social media, or other channels to get the word out?

- What types of publishers are they targeting with their promotions? Are they targeting a specific niche or a broad audience?

By analysing your competitors' promotions in this way, you can gain a better understanding of what types of promotions are most effective in your industry and tailor your own promotions accordingly. This can help you attract publishers and drive sales more effectively, ultimately leading to a more successful affiliate program.

Assess Affiliate Base

Assessing your competitors' affiliates can provide valuable insights into potential partners for your own affiliate program. By analysing their affiliate base, you can identify publishers that are likely to be interested in your program and develop strategies to attract them.

Take note of the types of publishers that are promoting your competitors' products or services. Are they niche bloggers, influencers, or large media outlets? What is their target audience, and how does it align with your brand's target market? Identifying these key characteristics can help you determine which publishers to target and how to tailor your program to their needs.

Additionally, analysing your competitors' affiliates can help you identify gaps in the market and find opportunities to attract new publishers. For example, if your competitors are primarily targeting bloggers in a certain niche, you may find opportunities to attract influencers or social media influencers who cater to the same audience.

By assessing your competitors' affiliates, you can develop a deeper understanding of the market and the types of publishers that are likely to be interested in your program.

Differentiate Your Program

Analysing your competitors' affiliate programs can help you identify areas where you can differentiate your program and stand out from the crowd. By offering something unique, you can attract publishers who are looking for something different and may be more likely to join your program.

One way to differentiate your program is by offering higher commission rates than your competitors. However, you need to make sure that you can still generate sustainable profitability while paying higher rates. Another way to differentiate your program is by offering exclusive promotions or products that are not available through your competitors' programs.

You can also differentiate your program by providing better support and communication to your publishers. By being responsive to their needs and providing them with the tools and resources they need to succeed, you can build strong relationships with your publishers and encourage them to promote your brand.

Finally, you can differentiate your program by focusing on a specific niche or vertical. By targeting a specific audience or industry, you can tailor your program to their specific needs and develop a reputation as a leader in that space. This can help you attract publishers who are interested in promoting products within that niche or industry.

Chapter 4: Choosing the Right Affiliate Network for Your Program - How It Can Affect Your Success

Choosing the right affiliate network to host your affiliate program is crucial to your program's success. The right network can provide you with the necessary tools and resources to launch and grow a successful program, while the wrong network can limit your program's potential and hinder your success. Here are some key factors to consider when choosing an affiliate network:

Network Reach

The size and reach of an affiliate network can have a significant impact on the potential success of your program. A larger network with more publishers can help you reach a wider audience and generate more sales, which is especially beneficial for brands that have a broad target audience. However, keep in mind that larger networks can also mean more competition for publishers' attention and less personal support.

On the other hand, a smaller network with more targeted publishers can also be effective, especially if your target audience is niche. A smaller network can offer more personalised support and attention, and may have stronger relationships with their publishers, allowing for more targeted promotions and higher conversion rates. Additionally, smaller networks often have lower fees and can be more flexible in terms of commission structures and program rules.

When choosing an affiliate network, consider the size and reach of the network in relation to your brand's target audience and the type of publishers you want to attract. Think about your goals for the program and what kind of support you'll need from the network to achieve them. Do you want a wide range of publishers and support with recruitment, or do you prefer a more personalised approach with dedicated account management?

Ultimately, the right network for your program will depend on your unique goals and needs, so take the time to research and compare different options before making a decision.

Commission Rates and Fees

When it comes to choosing the right affiliate network for your program, one of the most important factors to consider is the commission rates and fees that the network charges. Commission rates determine how much of a commission you will pay to your publishers for each sale or conversion they generate for your program. Meanwhile, fees can include everything from setup and network fees to additional fees for services such as program management, reporting, and fraud protection.

It's crucial to find an affiliate network that offers commission rates that are competitive within the market and align with your program's budget and profitability goals. Some networks may offer higher commission rates but also charge higher fees, while others may have lower commission rates but more reasonable fees. Ultimately, you'll need to strike a balance between commission rates and fees to ensure that your program is profitable and sustainable in the long run.

In addition to commission rates and fees, you'll also want to consider the payment terms and schedule of the affiliate network you choose. Make sure you understand the payment process and timeline, as well as any minimum payment thresholds or other requirements. You'll also want to ensure that the network offers reliable payment methods and has a good track record of paying publishers on time.

Finally, it's important to consider the level of support and resources that an affiliate network offers. Look for a network that provides robust reporting and analytics tools, fraud protection, and other features that can help you manage your program more effectively. You'll also want to ensure that the network has a knowledgeable and responsive support team that can help you address any issues or concerns that arise.

Affiliate Recruitment and Screening

Affiliate recruitment and screening are critical aspects of an affiliate program, and choosing the right affiliate network can greatly impact the success of these efforts. Some affiliate networks provide tools and resources for affiliate recruitment and screening, while others leave this up to the program manager.

Effective affiliate recruitment requires identifying and attracting publishers who are aligned with your brand and can promote your products or services to their audience effectively. A network with strong publisher relationships can help you identify potential partners, communicate with them effectively, and build long-term relationships.

Affiliate screening is equally important to ensure that you're working with high-quality partners who can deliver results for your program. A network that provides robust screening tools and processes can help you weed out publishers who are not a good fit for your program, such as those who engage in fraudulent activity or who do not meet your program requirements.

When choosing an affiliate network, it's important to consider the level of support they offer for affiliate recruitment and screening. A network with strong publisher relationships, effective communication tools, and robust screening processes can help you build a high-performing affiliate program that delivers sustainable results. On the other hand, a network that doesn't offer these services can lead to poor program performance and wasted resources.

Program Management Tools

Program management tools are essential for running a successful affiliate program, and the right network can provide you with the tools you need to manage and optimise your program effectively. It's important to choose a network that provides tools for tracking and reporting, managing affiliate relationships, and optimising performance.

Effective tracking and reporting tools are critical for understanding the performance of your affiliate program. Look for a network that provides real-time reporting on key metrics such as clicks, conversions, and commissions earned. This will help you identify which publishers are performing well and which ones may need additional support or attention.

Another important program management tool is the ability to manage affiliate relationships. This includes communication tools that allow you to easily communicate with publishers, as well as tools for managing commissions, payments, and other program-related tasks. A network that provides these tools can help streamline program management and ensure that everything runs smoothly.

Optimising performance is also key to running a successful affiliate program, and the right network can provide you with the tools you need to do this effectively. Look for a network that offers tools for split testing, A/B testing, and other optimisation strategies. This can help you identify which strategies are most effective and refine your program over time to improve performance.

Network Reputation

Network Reputation is an important consideration when choosing the right affiliate network for your program. A network with a strong reputation can help build trust with publishers, increase the credibility of your program, and attract more high-quality affiliates. Conversely, partnering with a network that has a poor reputation can result in a negative impact on your program's success and the quality of affiliates that you attract.

When evaluating network reputation, there are several factors to consider. Firstly, look at the network's track record of success. Have they worked with successful affiliate programs in the past? Are they known for providing effective support to their clients? You can research this by reading reviews and feedback from other program managers who have worked with the network in the past.

It's also important to consider the quality of the network's technology and resources. Does the network have a user-friendly interface that is easy to navigate? Are there effective tools for tracking and reporting program performance? The quality of these resources can have a significant impact on the success of your program, so it's important to choose a network with a good reputation in these areas.

Finally, consider the network's relationships with publishers. Do they have a strong network of quality publishers who are active in the affiliate space? Are they known for providing effective resources and support to these publishers? A network that has strong relationships with quality publishers can help ensure that your program attracts the best possible affiliates.

In summary, the reputation of the affiliate network you choose is an important consideration when setting up your program. A network with a strong reputation can help build trust with publishers, provide effective support and resources, and attract high-quality affiliates, all of which can contribute to the success of your program.

Chapter 5: Identifying Your Target Affiliate Partners - Finding the Right Fit for Your Brand

To launch a successful affiliate program, it's important to identify the right affiliate partners who align with your brand values and goals. Here are some key steps to identifying your target affiliate partners:

Define Your Target Audience

Defining your target audience is crucial when it comes to identifying your target affiliate partners. You need to have a clear understanding of your ideal customer persona, which includes their demographics, interests, and behaviours. This information will help you target publishers who have an audience that aligns with your target audience.

To define your target audience, consider factors such as age, gender, income level, geographic location, education level, interests, and purchasing behaviour. By understanding who your target audience is, you can identify the types of publishers who are likely to have an audience that matches your target audience.

For example, if your target audience is young, tech-savvy, and interested in gaming, you may want to target publishers who produce content related to gaming and technology. By doing so, you can reach an audience that is more likely to be interested in your brand and its products or services.

Once you have a clear understanding of your target audience, you can begin to identify the types of publishers who are most likely to reach that audience. This may include bloggers, influencers, content creators, or other types of publishers who produce content that is relevant to your target audience.

In addition to identifying the types of publishers who are likely to reach your target audience, you should also consider the types of promotions and incentives that are most likely to appeal to your target audience. This may include discounts, exclusive offers, or other types of incentives that are tailored to the interests and behaviours of your target audience.

Research Potential Publishers

Researching potential publishers is a crucial step in finding the right fit for your affiliate program. It is important to research potential publishers thoroughly to ensure that they align with your brand values and goals. Look for affiliates that have a strong online reputation, high-quality content, and an engaged audience. You can also use social media platforms to find potential partners and get a sense of their audience and engagement levels.

Additionally, it is important to consider the size and reach of potential publishers. Larger publishers may have a wider audience and reach, but smaller publishers may have a more targeted audience that aligns more closely with your target audience. Larger publisher may also be looking for higher commission rates compared to smaller publisher who will most likely accept your affiliate program default commission rate. It is important to find affiliates that have an audience that matches your target audience and that are likely to be interested in promoting your products or services.

Other methods of sourcing and researching potential publishers includes reaching out to close business connections and partners, asking them about their experiences in the affiliate marketing industry and if there are any publishers, they would recommend for you. You could even ask for an introduction.

Another benefit of launching your program through an affiliate network is you will most likely be assigned an account manager. The level of involvement, influence and support they have on your program varies from network to network, some networks also offer different levels of account management from basic support to fully managing you program. In most cases, your affiliate network will at least be able to point you in the right direction and could suggest publishers that would work well for your program. It is in the best interests of the network to generate sales for your brand so it is likely they will be able to support you in some capacity with researching potential publishers. The majority of networks also have a directory of publishers you can browse through and invite to your program, publishers will have a profile you can view, and you may also be able to search through and filter publishers based on certain factors such as categories e.g 'retail', publisher type e.g 'content' or country.

Assess Affiliate Compatibility

Assessing the compatibility of potential affiliate partners with your brand and program goals is an essential step in finding the right fit for your program. It's important to ensure that the affiliates you choose to work with are aligned with your brand values, have a similar target audience, and are using promotional methods that are suitable for your product or service.

One way to assess compatibility is to review the potential partner's website or social media channels to understand their audience demographics, content focus, and promotional tactics. You can also reach out to them directly to learn more about their promotional strategies and how they align with your goals.

Additionally, it's important to consider the reputation of potential partners in the industry. Look for affiliates who have a positive reputation and a history of promoting products or services similar to yours. You can also check industry forums and social media groups to see what other businesses are saying about working with these affiliates.

Ultimately, finding affiliates who are compatible with your brand and program goals can help ensure that you're working with partners who are most likely to drive results for your program. By taking the time to assess compatibility, you can build a network of trusted partners who are invested in the success of your program.

Establish Communication

Establishing communication with potential affiliate partners is a crucial step in building successful partnerships. Once you have identified potential publishers and assessed their compatibility with your brand, it's time to reach out and start building relationships.

One effective way to establish communication is through email outreach. Create a personalised email that introduces yourself, your brand, and your affiliate program. In the email, explain how your brand aligns with the publisher's audience and promotional methods, and highlight the benefits of joining your program. Be sure to keep the email concise, informative, and professional.

Social media is another effective channel to reach out to potential publishers. Follow them on social media platforms and engage with their content by liking, commenting, and sharing. This will help build brand awareness and create a connection between your brand and the publisher. Once you have built a relationship, you can direct message them and introduce your affiliate program.

When reaching out, it's important to establish a clear line of communication and provide support to potential publishers. Be responsive and helpful in answering their questions and addressing their concerns. This will help build trust and show that you are committed to creating a successful partnership.

Establishing communication is just the first step in building successful affiliate partnerships. It's important to continue nurturing these relationships through regular communication, providing support, and offering incentives for performance. By doing so, you can build a strong network of partners that can help drive sales and grow your business.

Evaluate Performance

Evaluating the performance of your affiliate partners is crucial to the success of your program. Tracking their performance allows you to identify which partners are driving the most traffic and conversions, and which ones may not be performing as well.

To evaluate performance, you'll need to establish key performance indicators (KPIs) that align with your program goals. Some common KPIs for affiliate programs include click-through rates (CTR), conversion rates, average order value (AOV), and revenue generated.

Use affiliate management software or tools provided by your affiliate network to track these KPIs for each partner. This will allow you to identify top-performing partners and those who may need additional support or guidance.

In addition to tracking performance metrics, it's important to communicate regularly with your affiliates. Ask for feedback and listen to their suggestions for improving the program. This will help you build stronger relationships with your partners and ultimately drive better results.

Based on your evaluation of performance, you may need to adjust your targeting and communication strategies. For example, if you notice that certain affiliates are performing well with a particular audience segment, you may want to adjust your targeting to focus on that segment.

Overall, regularly evaluating your affiliate partners' performance and making adjustments as needed is essential to the success of your program.

Chapter 6: Crafting Your Affiliate Program - Setting Goals, Establishing Terms, and Setting Up Your Affiliate Platform

Crafting an effective affiliate program requires careful planning and execution to ensure that your brand and affiliate partners can benefit from the partnership. Here are some key steps to crafting your affiliate program:

Set Clear Goals

Setting clear goals for your affiliate program is essential to ensure that you are on track to achieving your desired outcomes. When setting your goals, it's important to consider what you want to achieve and how you want to achieve it.

First, identify the specific objectives you want to accomplish with your affiliate program. These objectives should be specific, measurable, achievable, relevant, and time-bound (SMART). For instance, if you want to drive website traffic, consider setting a goal for the number of visits you want to generate.

Next, determine the metrics you will use to measure your success. Depending on your goals, these metrics may include website traffic, leads generated, sales made, or customer acquisition costs.

It's also important to consider the timeframe for achieving your goals. Setting a deadline can help you stay focused and motivated to achieve your desired outcomes.

Establish Program Terms

As you establish your affiliate program, it's important to define the terms and conditions that will govern your relationships with your publishers. These terms should include commission rates, payment terms, promotional guidelines, and any other rules that you want your publishers to follow.

Commission rates should be set based on industry standards and what you can afford as a business. It's important to strike a balance between offering competitive rates that will attract publishers and ensuring that your program remains profitable. Payment terms should also be clearly defined, including how often publishers will be paid and what payment methods will be accepted.

Promotional guidelines should outline the types of promotions that are allowed and what restrictions, if any, there are on how your brand can be promoted. For example, you may have specific requirements around the use of your brand logo or the types of content that can be used in promotions.

It's also important to comply with laws and regulations that govern affiliate marketing in your country of residence. In the UK, affiliate marketing is subject to the Advertising Standards Authority (ASA) guidelines, which require affiliates to disclose their relationship with the brand they are promoting. Failure to comply with these guidelines can result in fines or legal action.

Choose an Affiliate Network

Choosing an affiliate network is an essential step in setting up your affiliate program. When choosing a network, you need to consider various factors such as network reach, commission rates, network reputation, program management tools, and more.

There are several affiliate networks available that have a global presence, including Awin, Commission Junction, Rakuten Marketing, and others. Each network has its own strengths and weaknesses, so it's important to do your research and choose a platform that meets your specific needs and budget.

Awin is one of the most popular affiliate networks in the UK. It has a vast network of publishers and advertisers, making it an excellent choice for brands looking to reach a broad audience. Awin provides a range of tools and resources to help you manage your program effectively, including tracking and reporting tools, program management tools, and more.

Commission Junction, also known as CJ Affiliate, is another popular affiliate network in the UK. It has a broad network of publishers and advertisers, making it an excellent choice for brands looking to reach a large audience. Commission Junction offers a range of tools and resources to help you manage your program effectively, including tracking and reporting tools, program management tools, and more.

Rakuten Marketing is another popular affiliate network in the UK. It has a vast network of publishers and advertisers and offers a range of tools and resources to help you manage your program effectively. Rakuten Marketing also offers a range of commission rates, making it an excellent choice for brands with varying commission structures.

When choosing an affiliate network, it's important to consider your program goals and budget. Some networks may charge higher fees, but they may offer more resources and tools to help you manage your program effectively. On the other hand, some networks may be more affordable but may not offer the same level of resources and support.

Ultimately, the affiliate network you choose will play a significant role in the success of your affiliate program, so it's essential to do your research and choose a platform that meets your needs and budget.

Develop Marketing Materials

Developing marketing materials that are high-quality, visually appealing, and aligned with your brand identity is crucial for the success of your affiliate program. Publishers will be promoting your brand and products to their audience, so it's important to provide them with marketing materials that will effectively showcase your products and services.

Start by creating a set of branding guidelines that outline the colours, fonts, and visual elements that should be used in your marketing materials. This will ensure consistency across all your marketing collateral and help to reinforce your brand identity.

Next, create a range of marketing materials that publishers can use to promote your brand, such as banners, product images, and promotional text. Make sure these materials are optimised for different platforms and formats, such as social media, email, and website banners.

The most commonly used affiliate banner advert sizes are:

- Medium Rectangle (300x250 pixels)
- Leaderboard (728x90 pixels)
- Wide Skyscraper (160x600 pixels)
- Large Rectangle (336x280 pixels)
- Half Page (300x600 pixels)
- Billboard (970x250 pixels)
- Square (250x250 pixels)
- Skyscraper (120x600 pixels)

- Vertical Rectangle (240x400 pixels)
- Button (125x125 pixels)

It's also a good idea to create a landing page specifically for your affiliate program, where publishers can access all the marketing materials and resources they need to promote your brand effectively. This landing page should include clear calls-to-action, product information, and any relevant program terms and conditions.

Finally, regularly review and update your marketing materials to ensure they remain relevant and effective. Consider using A/B testing to test different marketing messages and designs, and use analytics to measure the performance of your marketing materials and make data-driven decisions about how to optimise your program.

Provide Affiliate Support

Offer support to your publishers by providing them with access to your marketing materials and offering guidance on best practices for promoting your brand. Consider setting up a support email address to help publishers with any questions or issues. Providing this level of support will help to build a stronger relationship with your affiliates and create a more successful program overall.

In addition to setting up a support email address, consider creating a comprehensive affiliate resource center. This center could include things such as guidelines on how to use your brand's messaging and logos, tips for creating effective content, and best practices for promoting your products or services. By providing your affiliates with a one-stop-shop for all of their resources, you'll make it easier for them to promote your brand effectively.

Another way to provide affiliate support is to offer personalised guidance and coaching. This could involve one-on-one consultations, group webinars, or access to a dedicated affiliate manager who can help answer any questions or provide support as needed. By offering this type of support, you'll help your affiliates to succeed in promoting your brand, which will ultimately benefit your business.

To ensure that your affiliate program is successful, it's also important to establish clear communication channels. Make it easy for your affiliates to reach out to you by establishing clear communication channels. This could include setting up a support email address, creating a dedicated section on your website for affiliates, or offering a phone number that affiliates can call for support. By making it easy for your affiliates to get in touch, you'll create a more positive and supportive environment.

Finally, consider establishing a feedback loop with your affiliates. Ask for feedback on your marketing materials, commission rates, and any other aspect of your program. By listening to your affiliates and acting on their feedback, you'll create a stronger relationship with them and improve the overall success of your program. Remember, a successful affiliate program is a partnership between you and your publishers, so be sure to provide the support they need to succeed.

Chapter 7: Recruiting and Onboarding Publishers - Best Practices for Finding and Welcoming New Partners to Your Program

Recruiting and onboarding new affiliates is an ongoing process that requires consistent effort to ensure that your affiliate program is successful. Here are some best practices for recruiting and onboarding affiliates to your program:

Create an Affiliate Program Landing Page

Create a dedicated landing page on your website that outlines the benefits of your affiliate program and provides clear instructions on how to join. This page could include information about commission rates, payment terms, and promotional guidelines. Having a dedicated landing page is an effective way to attract potential publishers and provide them with all the information they need to decide if your program is a good fit for them.

To make your landing page stand out, consider adding visuals such as images or videos that showcase your products or services. You could also include testimonials from existing publishers who have found success with your program. By showcasing the success of others, you can help potential publishers to envision their own success as part of your program.

Another important element to include on your landing page is a clear call-to-action (CTA). This could be a button that says 'Join Now' or 'Sign Up Today.' By making it easy for potential publishers to take the next step, you'll increase the likelihood of attracting new partners to your program. Make sure the CTA is prominently displayed on your landing page and is easy to find.

In addition to creating a landing page, consider promoting your program on social media and other relevant platforms. This could include posting about your program on your brand's social media channels, joining affiliate marketing groups on LinkedIn or Facebook, or partnering with industry influencers to promote your program. By spreading the word about your program, you'll increase your reach and attract new publishers who may not have otherwise heard about your program.

Overall, creating a dedicated landing page for your affiliate program is an effective way to attract potential publishers and provide them with the information they need to decide if your program is a good fit for them. By including information about commission rates, payment terms, and promotional guidelines, as well as visuals and testimonials, you'll increase the likelihood of attracting new partners to your program. Remember to include a clear call-to-action and to promote your program on social media and other relevant platforms to maximise your reach.

Attend Industry Events

Attend industry events and conferences to network with potential publishers and promote your program. This is a great opportunity to establish relationships with publishers and showcase your brand and program to a wider audience. Make a list of events that are relevant to your industry and affiliate program, and consider attending as many as possible throughout the year.

When attending events, be prepared to speak about your affiliate program and what makes it unique. You should also bring marketing materials, such as brochures or flyers, to distribute to potential publishers. These materials should highlight the benefits of your program and provide clear instructions on how to join.

In addition to attending industry events, consider hosting your own events, such as webinars or workshops, to promote your affiliate program. This is a great way to provide potential publishers with more information about your program and establish yourself as a thought leader in your industry. You could also offer special promotions or discounts to attendees who sign up for your program during the event.

Another way to network with potential publishers is to partner with other brands in your industry. This could include co-hosting events or collaborating on marketing campaigns. By partnering with other brands, you'll increase your reach and attract new publishers who may not have otherwise heard about your program.

Overall, attending industry events is a great way to network with potential publishers and promote your affiliate program. By being prepared to speak about your program, bringing marketing materials, and hosting your own events, you'll increase your chances of attracting new partners to your program. Don't forget to partner with other brands in your industry to increase your reach and establish yourself as a thought leader.

Offer Incentives

Offer incentives to attract new publishers, such as higher commission rates for a limited time or exclusive promotional materials. These incentives can help to differentiate your program from others and attract publishers who may be on the fence about joining. When offering incentives, be sure to clearly communicate the terms and conditions, including the start and end dates of the promotion.

Another way to offer incentives is to create a tiered commission structure that rewards publishers for reaching certain milestones, such as a higher commission rate for publishers who generate more than a certain number of sales per month. This can encourage publishers to promote your brand more actively and can help to establish a sense of healthy competition among your affiliates.

In addition to commission-based incentives, consider offering bonuses or rewards for top-performing publishers. This can help to motivate publishers to achieve better results and can help to establish a sense of community and camaraderie within your program. Rewards could include cash bonuses, gift cards, or even trips or experiences.

When offering incentives, be sure to communicate regularly with your publishers to keep them updated on their progress and any changes to the incentive program. This can help to keep your publishers engaged and motivated to promote your brand. It's also important to track the results of your incentive program and adjust it as necessary to ensure that it's effective in attracting and retaining high-quality publishers.

Overall, offering incentives is a great way to attract new publishers to your affiliate program and motivate existing publishers to promote your brand more actively. By creating a tiered commission structure, offering bonuses and rewards, and communicating regularly with your publishers, you'll establish a strong community of high-performing affiliates who are motivated to help grow your brand.

Provide Onboarding Support

Once you've recruited new publishers, provide onboarding support to ensure a smooth transition into the program. This includes providing access to marketing materials and offering guidance on how to promote your brand effectively. A successful onboarding process can help to establish a strong foundation for a long-term, productive relationship with your publishers.

One effective way to provide onboarding support is to create a welcome packet or series of emails that outline the key features of your program, including commission rates, promotional guidelines, and important dates or deadlines. This can help new publishers to get up to speed quickly and start promoting your brand as soon as possible.

In addition to written resources, consider hosting a live onboarding session, such as a webinar or conference call, where you can provide an overview of your program and answer any questions that new publishers may have. This can help to establish a personal connection with your publishers and create a sense of community within your program.

When providing onboarding support, it's important to be responsive to new publishers' needs and questions. Consider setting up a dedicated email address or phone line for onboarding inquiries, and assign a dedicated team member to manage this channel. This can help to ensure that new publishers feel supported and valued from the outset.

Overall, providing onboarding support is a crucial step in building a successful affiliate program. By creating resources such as welcome packets and hosting live onboarding sessions, and being responsive to new publishers' needs, you can establish a strong foundation for a long-term, productive relationship with your affiliates.

Communicate Regularly

Regularly communicate with your publishers to keep them engaged and informed about program updates, promotional opportunities, and other important information. Effective communication is a key factor in maintaining a strong and productive relationship with your affiliates.

One effective way to communicate regularly with your publishers is to send out a regular newsletter or email update. This could include information about new products or services, upcoming promotions or sales, and other relevant program updates. Be sure to keep the tone friendly and approachable, and encourage your publishers to reach out with any questions or feedback.

In addition to regular email updates, consider hosting periodic webinars or Q&A sessions where you can provide updates and answer questions from your publishers in real-time. This can help to establish a personal connection with your affiliates and foster a sense of community within your program.

When communicating with your publishers, it's important to listen to their feedback and suggestions. Consider setting up a feedback channel or survey to solicit input from your affiliates about how you can improve your program and better support their efforts. This can help to create a more collaborative and productive relationship with your publishers.

Overall, regular communication is a critical component of a successful affiliate program. By providing regular updates and opportunities for feedback, you can keep your publishers engaged and motivated, and establish a productive and mutually beneficial relationship with your affiliates.

Chapter 8: Optimising Your Affiliate Program - Measuring Performance, Identifying Opportunities, and Adjusting Strategies

To ensure that your affiliate program remains successful in the long term, it's important to continually optimise it based on performance data and industry trends. Here are some key steps to optimising your affiliate program:

Track Performance Metrics

Use analytics tools to track key performance metrics, such as clicks, conversions, and revenue generated by your publishers. Use this data to identify areas of your program that are performing well and areas that need improvement. This information can help you optimise your program and make data-driven decisions to maximise your return on investment.

One important metric to track is the conversion rate of your affiliates. This measures the percentage of clicks that result in a sale or other desired action, such as signing up for a newsletter or filling out a contact form. By tracking conversion rates, you can identify which publishers are driving the most valuable traffic to your site and adjust your commission rates and promotional strategies accordingly.

Another important metric to track is the revenue generated by your affiliates. This measures the total amount of sales or revenue generated by your publishers. By tracking revenue, you can identify which publishers are the most valuable to your program and adjust your promotional strategies to focus on these top-performing affiliates.

In addition to tracking conversion rates and revenue, be sure to also monitor other key performance indicators such as click-through rates, average order value, and customer lifetime value. By analysing these metrics, you can gain a more comprehensive understanding of how your program is performing and identify areas for improvement.

Overall, tracking performance metrics is a critical component of optimising your affiliate program. By using data to inform your decisions and identify areas for improvement, you can make strategic adjustments to your program that will drive more traffic, sales, and revenue for your business.

Identify Opportunities for Improvement

Based on your performance data, identify opportunities for improvement in your affiliate program. This could include adjusting commission rates, updating marketing materials, or targeting new publishers. By continuously evaluating your program's performance and making strategic adjustments, you can optimise your program for maximum success.

One opportunity for improvement may be to adjust your commission rates. If certain publishers are driving a large volume of traffic but not generating many sales, you may want to consider increasing their commission rate to incentivise them to promote your brand more effectively. On the other hand, if certain publishers are generating a high volume of sales but not driving much traffic, you may want to adjust their commission rate to better reflect the value they are bringing to your program.

Another opportunity for improvement may be to update your marketing materials. If you notice that certain promotional materials are not performing well, you may want to test new creative assets to see if they drive better results. Additionally, you may want to provide publishers with new marketing materials to keep their promotions fresh and relevant.

Lastly, consider targeting new publishers to expand your program's reach. Look for publishers in your niche who have a strong following or a high level of engagement with their audience. By partnering with these publishers and providing them with the resources they need to promote your brand effectively, you can tap into new sources of traffic and revenue for your business.

Adjust Program Strategies

Use the insights gained from performance data and industry trends to adjust your program strategies. This may involve experimenting with new promotional methods, refining your target audience, or adjusting your commission structure. It's important to continually optimise your program to ensure that it remains competitive and effective.

One way to adjust your program strategies is by experimenting with different promotional methods. For example, you could test out different types of content, such as blog posts, social media posts, or video tutorials. You could also try running different types of promotions, such as limited-time offers or exclusive discounts for your affiliate partners.

Refining your target audience can also help improve the effectiveness of your program. Consider the demographics and interests of your existing customers and try to target publishers who have an audience that aligns with your brand. By doing so, you can increase the likelihood that your affiliate partners' promotions will resonate with their audience and drive more conversions.

Finally, adjusting your commission structure can help incentivise your publishers to perform better. Consider offering higher commission rates for top-performing publishers or increasing commission rates for certain products or services. By doing so, you can encourage your publishers to focus on promoting the products or services that have the highest earning potential.

Monitor Industry Trends

Stay up to date with industry trends and changes in the affiliate marketing landscape in your country of residence. This will help you stay ahead of the competition and make informed decisions about your program.

To run a successful affiliate program, it's crucial to stay current with the latest trends and shifts in the industry. By doing so, you'll have a better understanding of the challenges and opportunities that exist, and can make data-driven decisions to adjust your program accordingly. Regularly monitoring industry trends will also help you stay ahead of the competition, as you'll be able to quickly adapt to any changes in the marketplace.

One way to stay up to date with industry trends is to subscribe to industry publications, such as Affiliate Marketing Insider or PerformanceIN. These publications provide valuable insights into industry trends, as well as tips and strategies for running a successful affiliate program. You can also attend industry conferences and events, where you can network with peers, learn about emerging technologies and trends, and discover new ways to optimise your program.

In addition, keep an eye on changes in laws and regulations that may impact your affiliate program. For example, in the UK, the Advertising Standards Authority (ASA) regulates online advertising and requires all affiliate marketers to comply with certain guidelines. Being aware of any changes to these guidelines will ensure that your program remains compliant and avoids any potential legal issues.

Finally, be mindful of changes in consumer behaviour, as these can also impact your affiliate program. For example, shifts in the way people shop, the types of products they buy, or the devices they use to browse the internet can all have a significant impact on your program's performance. By monitoring these trends, you can adjust your program accordingly and stay ahead of the curve.

Provide Ongoing Support

Offering ongoing support to your publishers is crucial for maintaining a successful affiliate program. As your program grows and evolves, it's important to continue providing resources and support to help your publishers promote your brand effectively. This includes providing access to marketing materials and offering guidance on best practices for promotion.

Additionally, responding to questions or concerns in a timely manner is crucial for keeping your publishers engaged and satisfied. Consider setting up a dedicated support email address or chat service that publishers can use to reach out with any questions or issues. Responding promptly to these inquiries will demonstrate your commitment to your publishers and help build trust and loyalty.

Another way to offer ongoing support is to regularly provide your publishers with updates on program performance, promotional opportunities, and other important information. This could include regular newsletters or webinars that provide tips and strategies for promoting your brand effectively.

Finally, don't be afraid to ask your publishers for feedback on how to improve your program. This can help you identify areas where you may be falling short and make necessary improvements to ensure the ongoing success of your program. By working closely with your publishers and providing ongoing support, you can create a thriving affiliate program that benefits both your brand and your publishers.

Chapter 9: Maintaining Compliance - Staying Up-to-Date on Regulations and Best Practices for Affiliate Marketing

Affiliate marketing is subject to various laws and regulations, in the UK this includes the Advertising Standards Authority's (ASA) regulations on advertising and the General Data Protection Regulation (GDPR). To ensure that your affiliate program is compliant with these regulations, here are some best practices to follow:

Review ASA Guidelines

Familiarise yourself with the Advertising Standards Authority (ASA) guidelines on advertising, which set out the requirements for clear and truthful advertising and transparency regarding paid endorsements. As an affiliate marketer in the UK, it's essential to understand and comply with these guidelines to avoid penalties and damage to your brand's reputation.

Review the specific requirements of the ASA's CAP Code, which covers all non-broadcast media. This code requires that all marketing communications are clearly identifiable as such and do not mislead the audience. Additionally, all paid endorsements must be clearly identified as such, and affiliate marketers must ensure that any claims made about products or services are accurate and can be substantiated.

Ensure that your publishers are aware of these guidelines and are also compliant with them. Provide them with guidance on how to create truthful and transparent advertising content, and monitor their content regularly to ensure that it meets the ASA's requirements.

Stay up-to-date with any changes or updates to the ASA guidelines, as they may evolve over time to reflect new practices or technologies. Attend relevant training or events to learn more about these changes and how they may impact your affiliate marketing program.

By adhering to the ASA guidelines, you can ensure that your affiliate marketing program is ethical, transparent, and compliant with regulations. This will not only protect your brand's reputation but also build trust with your audience and ultimately drive better results for your business.

Obtain Consent for Data Collection

Obtaining explicit consent for data collection is an essential aspect of maintaining compliance in affiliate marketing. With data privacy regulations becoming more stringent, it's important to ensure that your customers are fully informed about how their data is being collected and used by your program.

To obtain consent, it's important to provide clear and concise information about the types of data that will be collected, how the data will be used, and any third-party entities that will have access to the data. This information should be provided in a prominent location on your website, such as a privacy policy or terms of service agreement.

Additionally, you should make it easy for customers to opt-out of data collection activities, such as cookie tracking. This could involve offering a clear and visible opt-out button or link on your website, or providing instructions on how to disable cookies in their browser settings.

By obtaining explicit consent and making it easy for customers to opt-out, you can help ensure that your program is in compliance with your country of residence regulations and best practices for data privacy. This will help protect your brand's reputation and build trust with your customers and publishers.

Use Secure Payment Systems

Use secure payment systems to protect your brand and your publishers from fraud, and to ensure that payments are processed securely. Fraudulent activity is a risk in any online transaction, so it's important to choose a reliable payment system with strong security measures in place. Make sure to research and choose a payment system that is trustworthy, secure, and compatible with your affiliate program platform.

A secure payment system will not only protect your brand and publishers from fraud but also provide peace of mind for all parties involved. By choosing a reliable and secure payment system, you'll ensure that all transactions are processed smoothly and efficiently, without any glitches or delays. This can help build trust with your publishers and encourage them to continue promoting your brand.

In addition to choosing a secure payment system, it's also important to establish clear payment terms with your publishers. Be transparent about commission rates, payment schedules, and any other relevant information. This will help build trust with your publishers and avoid any misunderstandings or disputes down the line.

Remember that providing secure payment options is not just a legal requirement, but it's also a best practice that can benefit your brand and your publishers in the long run. By using a secure payment system and establishing clear payment terms, you'll create a more transparent and trustworthy affiliate program that can attract and retain high-quality publishers.

Provide Clear Program Terms

Providing clear and transparent program terms is essential for maintaining compliance with regulations and ensuring that publishers understand their obligations within the program. This includes outlining commission rates, payment terms, and promotional guidelines in a clear and concise manner.

Commission rates should be clearly stated upfront and any changes to these rates should be communicated in a timely manner. Payment terms should also be clearly defined, including when and how publishers will be paid for their referrals.

In addition to commission rates and payment terms, it is important to provide clear guidelines for promotional activities. This includes outlining what is and isn't allowed when promoting the brand and the consequences for violating these guidelines.

By providing clear program terms, you can ensure that publishers understand their obligations within the program and avoid any potential violations. This not only helps to maintain compliance with regulations, but also promotes a positive and transparent relationship between your brand and your publishers.

Monitor Affiliate Activities

Regularly monitoring affiliate activities is an essential part of maintaining compliance in your affiliate program. By keeping a close eye on the activities of your publishers, you can ensure that they are adhering to your program terms and regulations, and take appropriate action if necessary to address any issues that arise.

One way to monitor affiliate activities is to use tracking software that can provide detailed data on clicks, conversions, and other metrics. This can help you identify any publishers who are engaging in fraudulent or non-compliant activities, such as incentivising clicks or using misleading advertising.

Another important aspect of monitoring affiliate activities is to keep a close eye on the content that publishers are using to promote your brand. This includes ensuring that they are complying with advertising guidelines set out by organisations such as the Advertising Standards Authority (ASA), as well as ensuring that they are not engaging in any practices that could damage your brand reputation.

If you do identify any non-compliant activities by your publishers, it is important to take swift action to address the issue. This could involve issuing a warning, revoking commissions, or even terminating the publisher's participation in your program altogether.

By regularly monitoring affiliate activities and taking action when necessary, you can help ensure that your program remains compliant with regulations and best practices, and that your brand reputation remains strong.

Keep Up-to-Date with Regulatory Changes

To ensure that your affiliate program stays compliant with regulations, it's important to stay up-to-date with any changes in the regulatory landscape. Keep an eye on industry news and resources, and be aware of any new regulations or updates to existing regulations that may affect your program.

One way to stay informed is to subscribe to regulatory alerts or newsletters from relevant bodies, such as the Advertising Standards

Authority (ASA) or the Information Commissioner's Office (ICO). These organisations provide updates on changes to regulations, as well as guidance on best practices for compliance.

It's also important to regularly review your program policies and procedures to ensure they are compliant with current regulations. This includes your data privacy policy, terms and conditions, and any promotional guidelines or disclosure requirements.

If you identify any areas where your program may be out of compliance, take immediate action to address the issue. This may involve adjusting your program policies, providing additional training to your publishers, or making changes to your marketing materials or promotional strategies.

By staying up-to-date with regulatory changes and taking proactive steps to maintain compliance, you can help ensure that your affiliate program is operating in accordance with regulations and best practices. This can help protect your brand and your publishers, and promote trust and transparency in the affiliate marketing industry.

Chapter 10: Managing Affiliate Relationships - Building Strong Partnerships and Resolving Conflicts

Effective affiliate program management involves building strong relationships with your publishers and resolving any conflicts that may arise. Here are some best practices for managing affiliate relationships:

Provide Clear Guidelines

To build strong affiliate partnerships, it is important to provide clear guidelines to your publishers. These guidelines should cover a range of important program details, such as promotional methods, product usage, and compliance requirements. By providing clear instructions, you can prevent misunderstandings and ensure that publishers are promoting your brand effectively.

One of the key aspects of providing clear guidelines is outlining the promotional methods that are allowed within your program. This could include specifying which channels are acceptable for promoting your brand, as well as any restrictions on messaging or creative assets. Additionally, providing publishers with guidance on how to use your products or services effectively can help ensure that their promotions are accurate and aligned with your brand's messaging.

Another important area to cover in your guidelines is compliance requirements. This could include guidelines related to the ASA guidelines on advertising, data collection, and disclosure of paid endorsements. By clearly outlining your program's requirements, you can ensure that your publishers are staying compliant and avoid any potential legal issues.

In addition to providing clear guidelines, it's important to offer ongoing support and guidance to your publishers. This could include regular communication and check-ins, as well as access to marketing materials and other resources. By providing support, you can help your publishers succeed and build stronger relationships with them over time.

Offer Incentives

Offering incentives is a powerful way to motivate affiliates to promote your brand more effectively. By providing rewards for top-performing publishers, you can encourage them to invest more time and effort into promoting your products or services. One effective incentive strategy is to offer exclusive discounts to affiliates that can be passed on to their audience. This not only incentivises affiliates to promote your brand but also provides added value to their audience, increasing the likelihood of conversions.

Another effective incentive strategy is to offer higher commission rates to top-performing publishers. By increasing commission rates for affiliates that consistently generate sales or leads, you can motivate them to continue promoting your brand and to invest more time and resources into promoting your products or services. This can be particularly effective in competitive industries where publishers may have multiple brands to choose from.

You can also consider offering bonuses or rewards for achieving specific performance goals. For example, you could offer a cash bonus for publishers that generate a certain number of sales within a given timeframe or offer prizes for the top-performing publishers in a particular promotion. This not only incentivises affiliates to promote your brand but also creates friendly competition among your publishers, which can lead to increased engagement and better results.

In addition to these strategies, you can also consider offering other benefits to your top-performing publishers, such as access to exclusive promotional materials, early access to new products or services, or dedicated account management support. By providing these additional benefits, you can create a sense of loyalty and partnership with your top-performing publishers, which can lead to a long-lasting and productive relationship.

However, it's important to ensure that your incentive program is fair and transparent. Make sure that all publishers have access to the same incentives and that the criteria for earning rewards is clearly communicated. You should also regularly review and adjust your incentive program based on performance data to ensure that it's effective and aligned with your overall goals.

Communicate Regularly

Communicating regularly with your publishers is key to building strong and productive relationships. Regular communication can help keep your publishers engaged and motivated to promote your brand effectively. It is important to keep your publishers informed about program updates, promotional opportunities, and other important information that may affect their participation in your program.

One effective way to communicate regularly with your publishers is to send out regular newsletters or emails. These communications can provide updates on new products or services, promotional opportunities, and important changes to the program. They can also highlight top-performing publishers and provide tips and best practices for promoting your brand effectively.

Another important aspect of regular communication is to be responsive to your publishers' needs and concerns. Encourage your publishers to reach out with any questions or issues they may have, and be sure to respond in a timely and helpful manner. This can help build trust and demonstrate that you value your publishers as partners in your program.

In addition to regular newsletters and emails, consider holding regular check-ins or webinars with your publishers. These sessions can provide an opportunity for you to share updates and answer questions, as well as for your publishers to share their experiences and best practices with each other.

Finally, be sure to listen to your publishers' feedback and suggestions for program improvements. Soliciting and implementing feedback from your publishers can help keep them engaged and invested in your program, and can also lead to improvements in program performance and effectiveness.

Address Conflicts Promptly

If conflicts do arise between you and your publishers, it's important to address them promptly and professionally. Ignoring conflicts or letting them fester can lead to damaged relationships and decreased productivity. Therefore, it's important to have a clear plan in place for how to handle conflicts before they occur.

When conflicts do arise, start by having a conversation with the publisher in question. Listen to their concerns and be open to their perspective. It's important to understand the root of the conflict and the reasons behind their actions. Once you have a clear understanding of the issue, work together to come up with a mutually beneficial solution.

Sometimes, conflicts arise due to misunderstandings or miscommunications. In these cases, it may be helpful to clarify your program guidelines or provide additional training to help prevent similar conflicts from occurring in the future.

In some cases, conflicts may arise due to a publisher violating program guidelines or engaging in fraudulent activities. In these cases, it's important to take swift action to protect your brand and other publishers in the program. This may involve terminating the publisher's participation in the program and taking legal action if necessary.

Regardless of the type of conflict, it's important to handle the situation with professionalism and respect. By working together to find a solution, you can help preserve your relationship with the publisher and maintain a positive reputation in the affiliate marketing community.

Provide Support and Resources

Offering support and resources to your publishers can go a long way in building strong partnerships and improving the performance of your affiliate program. By providing publishers with the tools and knowledge they need to promote your brand effectively, you can help them succeed and ultimately drive more revenue for your business.

One way to provide support is by giving publishers access to marketing materials such as banners, text links, and product images. This can save them time and effort in creating their own promotional content, and also ensure that the branding and messaging is consistent across all channels. Providing a variety of materials that cater to different marketing channels and audiences can also help publishers better tailor their campaigns to their specific audience.

Training on best practices is another way to support your publishers. This could include webinars, articles, and other resources that provide guidance on effective marketing strategies and compliance with program terms and regulations. Helping publishers understand how to optimise their campaigns can not only improve their performance but also prevent any potential issues that may arise from lack of knowledge.

Offering a dedicated email address or other form of support can also help publishers feel supported and valued. This allows them to reach out with questions, concerns, or feedback and receive a timely response. By being responsive and helpful, you can build stronger relationships with your publishers and foster a sense of partnership and trust.

Chapter 11: Scaling Your Affiliate Program - Expanding Your Program and Maximising Growth

As your affiliate program grows and becomes more successful, it's important to consider ways to scale the program and maximise growth. Here are some best practices for scaling your affiliate program:

Expand Your Publisher Base

Expanding your publisher base is a key strategy for scaling your affiliate program and maximising growth. There are several ways to approach this, including targeting new audiences or niches, reaching out to influencers, and leveraging social media platforms.

One way to expand your publisher base is by targeting new audiences or niches. This involves identifying new groups of potential customers who may be interested in your products or services but are not currently being reached through your existing publishers. For example, if you sell fitness products, you may want to consider partnering with publishers who cater to the yoga or running niches.

Another strategy is to reach out to influencers in your industry. Influencers have large followings on social media and can help promote your brand to their audience. This can be a particularly effective strategy for reaching younger audiences who are more likely to engage with social media influencers.

Social media platforms can also be a powerful tool for expanding your publisher base. By leveraging social media channels such as

Facebook, Twitter, and Instagram, you can reach a wider audience and connect with potential publishers who may be interested in promoting your brand. You can also use social media to engage with your existing publishers and provide them with additional support and resources.

In addition to expanding your publisher base, it's important to focus on maximising the performance of your existing publishers. This involves providing ongoing support, offering incentives and rewards for top-performing publishers, and regularly reviewing your program's performance metrics to identify areas for improvement.

Increase Commission Rates

One of the most effective ways to incentivise publishers to promote your brand more aggressively and attract new publishers to the program is by increasing commission rates. Higher commission rates can motivate publishers to put more effort into promoting your brand and can attract new publishers who are looking for higher earning potential. Additionally, higher commission rates can help you stay competitive within your industry and attract top-performing publishers.

When considering increasing commission rates, it's important to review your current financial situation and ensure that you can afford the increase. You should also consider the impact that increased commission rates will have on your profit margins and whether the potential benefits outweigh the costs. It's important to strike a balance between incentivising publishers and maintaining profitability.

Another factor to consider when increasing commission rates is the impact on your existing publishers. You'll want to ensure that your current publishers are not negatively affected by the increase and that they continue to be motivated to promote your brand. One way to mitigate this is by offering tiered commission rates based on performance, so that top-performing publishers receive a higher commission rate while new or lower-performing publishers start at a lower rate.

Offer Performance-Based Incentives

In addition to offering higher commission rates, one effective way to incentivise publishers to perform better and drive more traffic and sales to your brand is by offering performance-based incentives. These could be in the form of bonuses, exclusive rewards, or even special recognition for top-performing publishers. By offering such incentives, you can motivate publishers to work harder, improve their performance, and achieve better results.

When designing performance-based incentives, it is important to establish clear criteria for eligibility and determine what constitutes success. You may want to set benchmarks for the number of clicks, leads, or sales that publishers need to generate to qualify for the incentive. You may also want to consider setting performance goals for individual publishers based on their performance history and capabilities.

Another way to offer performance-based incentives is to provide tiered commission rates that increase as publishers meet specific performance targets. For example, you may offer a higher commission rate to publishers who generate a certain number of sales or leads per month. This approach can be effective in motivating publishers to achieve specific goals and can also help you maximise your return on investment.

It is important to keep in mind that offering performance-based incentives can be costly, and you will need to balance the benefits of incentivising publishers against the costs of doing so. You will also need to be transparent about the criteria for eligibility and the rewards offered to ensure that publishers understand what is required of them and are motivated to work towards the incentive.

In addition to financial incentives, you may also consider offering non-financial incentives, such as access to exclusive content, free products or services, or recognition for top-performing publishers. These types of incentives can be a powerful motivator for publishers and can help you build strong relationships with your top-performing affiliates.

Invest in Marketing and Advertising

Investing in marketing and advertising campaigns is an effective way to increase brand awareness and attract new customers to your website. By doing so, you can drive more traffic to your affiliate program and attract new publishers, ultimately helping you to scale your affiliate program and maximise growth.

One way to invest in marketing and advertising is through paid search and display advertising. With paid search, you can bid on keywords relevant to your brand and target specific demographics or geographic locations. Display advertising allows you to place ads on websites and social media platforms to reach your target audience. Both methods can help increase visibility and drive traffic to your website, ultimately leading to more conversions and revenue for your affiliate program.

Another way to invest in marketing and advertising is through content marketing. By creating high-quality, informative content such as blog posts, videos, or infographics, you can attract new customers to your website and establish your brand as a thought leader in your industry. You can also partner with influencers and bloggers to promote your content and affiliate program, increasing your reach and driving more traffic to your website.

Additionally, social media marketing can be a valuable tool in increasing brand awareness and driving traffic to your website. By creating engaging content and building a community on platforms such as Facebook, Instagram, and Twitter, you can attract new customers and promote your affiliate program to a wider audience. Social media can also be used to communicate with your publishers and provide updates on program changes or promotional opportunities.

Leverage Technology

Leveraging technology can be an effective way to streamline and automate various tasks involved in managing your affiliate program. By using technology tools, you can not only save time and effort but also improve the overall efficiency and effectiveness of your program.

One useful technology tool for affiliate program management is performance tracking software. This type of software allows you to track important metrics such as click-through rates, conversion rates, and revenue generated by each publisher. With this data, you can make informed decisions about which publishers to focus on, which promotional methods are most effective, and how to allocate resources for maximum impact.

Another important tool is marketing automation software, which can help you create and distribute marketing materials more efficiently. With automation software, you can create email campaigns, social media posts, and other promotional content that can be customised for individual publishers or groups of publishers. This can help you save time and ensure that your brand message is consistent across all channels.

Affiliate management platforms are also useful for managing your program more efficiently. These platforms allow you to track publisher performance, manage pay-outs, and monitor compliance with program terms and regulations. Additionally, some platforms provide tools for communication and collaboration with publishers, making it easier to provide support and resources to your partners.

Finally, consider using data analytics tools to gain insights into customer behaviour and preferences. By analysing data on customer demographics, purchasing habits, and other metrics, you can better understand your target audience and tailor your marketing efforts accordingly. This can help you identify new opportunities for growth and optimise your affiliate program for maximum results.

Chapter 12: Final Thoughts on Launching an Affiliate Program

Launching an affiliate program can be a highly effective way to drive traffic to your website, increase brand awareness, and generate revenue. However, to achieve success in the competitive affiliate market, it's important to follow best practices and continually optimise your program based on performance data and industry trends.

Throughout this book, we've covered key considerations for launching an affiliate program, including:

- Setting program goals and selecting the right platform
- Recruiting and evaluating potential publishers effectively
- Creating compelling marketing materials and promotions
- Optimising program performance and staying compliant with laws and regulations
- Managing affiliate relationships and scaling the program for growth

By following these best practices, you can launch an effective affiliate program and achieve your affiliate marketing goals.

Launching and managing a successful affiliate program takes time, effort, and dedication. But with the right strategies and tools, you can build a strong program that drives traffic, generates revenue, and enhances your brand's reputation in the market.

Glossary of Terms

Advertiser (Merchant or Brand)

An advertiser or merchant is a company or individual that sells products or services via their own affiliate program. The advertiser typically provides promotional materials, such as banner ads and text links, to affiliates who promote their products or services on their websites or other marketing channels. The advertiser pays the affiliates a commission for each sale or conversion that is generated through their unique affiliate link. The advertiser is responsible for setting commission rates, providing product or service information, and managing the affiliate program.

Affiliate Link (Deep Link)

An affiliate link is a unique URL provided to an affiliate by an advertiser or merchant that includes a tracking code. When a customer clicks on an affiliate's link and makes a purchase or performs a desired action, the tracking code in the URL is used to track the transaction and attribute it to the affiliate, allowing them to earn a commission for the sale or action. Affiliate links are a key component of affiliate marketing and are used to track the performance of individual affiliates and the overall success of an affiliate program.

Affiliate Network

An affiliate network is a platform that connects advertisers or merchants with a network of affiliates who promote their products or services in exchange for a commission. It serves as a middleman between advertisers and publishers, providing tools and resources to manage and track affiliate programs. Affiliate networks typically handle tasks such as tracking clicks and conversions, managing payments to affiliates, and providing support to both advertisers and publishers. They also often offer a variety of tools to help affiliates effectively promote the advertiser's products or services.

Affiliate (Publisher)

An affiliate, also known as a publisher, is an individual or company that promotes the products or services of an advertiser or merchant to their own audience. Affiliates earn a commission for every sale, lead, or click generated through their unique affiliate link.

Affiliates can be bloggers, social media influencers, website owners, or anyone with an online presence and a following. They use various marketing techniques such as content marketing, search engine optimisation, social media advertising, and email marketing to drive traffic to the advertiser's website and promote their products or services.

Affiliates can join affiliate programs through affiliate networks or directly with advertisers. They typically have access to a range of marketing materials, such as banners, text links, and product feeds, which they can use to promote the advertiser's products or services on their platform.

Affiliates play a crucial role in the success of an affiliate marketing program, as they are responsible for driving traffic and sales to the advertiser's website. In exchange, they receive a commission for every successful referral, making it a win-win situation for both the affiliate and the advertiser.

Affiliate Program

An affiliate program is a type of marketing program in which a business (the advertiser/merchant) partners with affiliates (publishers) to promote their products or services in exchange for a commission. The program provides the affiliates with unique affiliate links or codes that they can use to promote the advertiser's products or services to their own audience. When a user clicks on an affiliate link or code and completes a desired action (such as making a purchase), the affiliate earns a commission.

The affiliate program typically includes terms and conditions that govern the relationship between the advertiser/merchant and the affiliates. This can include commission rates, payment terms, promotional guidelines, and other important details. The advertiser/merchant may also provide marketing materials and resources to help the affiliates promote their products or services effectively.

Affiliate programs can be managed in-house by the advertiser/merchant or through an affiliate network, which acts as a middleman between the advertiser/merchant and the affiliates. Affiliate programs can be a cost-effective way for businesses to increase their reach and drive more sales, while providing affiliates with a source of passive income.

Commission

A commission refers to the compensation or payment that an affiliate receives for each successful referral or sale made through their unique affiliate link. The commission amount is typically a percentage of the sale value but can also be a fixed amount per sale or per lead generated. The commission rate is determined by the advertiser or merchant and is outlined in the affiliate program's terms and conditions. The commission serves as an incentive for affiliates to promote the advertiser's products or services to their audience.

Conversion rate

Conversion rate refers to the percentage of website visitors who complete a desired action, such as making a purchase, filling out a form, or subscribing to a newsletter. In affiliate marketing, conversion rate is a critical metric used to measure the success of a campaign or program. A higher conversion rate indicates that more visitors are completing the desired action, resulting in increased revenue for the advertiser and affiliate. Conversion rate can be affected by various factors, including website design, user experience, pricing, and product quality. Marketers often use conversion rate optimisation (CRO) techniques to improve the effectiveness of their campaigns and drive more conversions.

Cookies

A cookie is a small text file that is placed on a user's device (such as a computer or mobile phone) when they click on an affiliate link. This cookie contains information about the user's activity on the advertiser's website, including the date and time of their visit, the pages they viewed, and any actions they took, such as making a purchase.

Cookies are used by advertisers to track the activity of users who click on their affiliate links and attribute commissions to the appropriate affiliates. They are also used to help personalise the user experience and to provide targeted advertising.

The length of time that a cookie remains on a user's device varies depending on the affiliate program, but typically ranges from a few days to several months, the average is 30 days. If a user returns to the advertiser's website and completes a purchase within the cookie's lifespan, the affiliate who originally referred the user will receive a commission for that sale.

Cost per click (CPC)

Cost per click (CPC) is a pricing model used in affiliate marketing where advertisers pay affiliates based on the number of clicks generated by their affiliate links. This means that the advertiser pays the affiliate a fixed amount each time a user clicks on their affiliate link, regardless of whether or not the user makes a purchase on the advertiser's website. CPC is commonly used in search engine advertising and pay-per-click campaigns, and it allows advertisers to control their advertising costs more precisely by only paying for clicks that result in traffic to their website.

Earnings per click (EPC)

Earnings per click (EPC) is a metric used to measure the effectiveness of an affiliate marketing campaign. It is the average amount of commission earned per click on an affiliate link. EPC is calculated by dividing the total commission earned by the number of clicks generated by the affiliate link.

For example, if an affiliate link generates 1,000 clicks and earns £1,000 in commission, the EPC would be £1.00. EPC can vary depending on the product or service being promoted, the commission rate, and the effectiveness of the affiliate's marketing efforts.

EPC is a useful metric for both affiliates and merchants as it allows them to assess the performance of their affiliate marketing campaigns and make adjustments to improve their results. Affiliates can use EPC to identify the most profitable campaigns and focus their efforts on promoting those products or services, while merchants can use

EPC to evaluate the performance of their affiliate program and make changes to their commission rates or promotional materials as needed.

Return on investment (ROI)

Return on investment (ROI) is a metric used to measure the profitability of an investment relative to its cost. In affiliate marketing, ROI refers to the amount of revenue generated by an affiliate program compared to the cost of running the program, including the cost of paying commissions to affiliates, marketing and advertising expenses, and other associated costs.

ROI can be calculated using the following formula: (Revenue - Cost) / Cost x 100%. A positive ROI indicates that the program is profitable, while a negative ROI indicates that the program is not generating enough revenue to cover its costs.

ROI is an important metric in affiliate marketing as it helps advertisers and merchants evaluate the effectiveness of their affiliate program and make decisions on how to allocate their resources. A high ROI indicates that the program is successful in driving sales and generating revenue, while a low ROI may indicate that adjustments need to be made to the program to improve its performance.